The Purpose of Emotions

From Self-defeat to Fulfillment

Table of Contents

Preface

Who should read this book?

This book is for anyone stressed by emotions – being pushed and pulled, surprised, troubled by and knocked about by them. Yes, I'm referring to anger, hurt, depression, anxiety, loneliness, insecurity, rejection and more. It is also for those who want to understand their emotional moods that surround, capture and threaten to bury you. You will find immediate use for the energy and direction contained in all the major emotions – all 14 of them. You will be relieved to find they are your friends and are on your side.

This book is also for counselors, psychologists, social workers, teachers, and anyone who has a close relation that needs their attention. Emotions have been the stepchild in psychotherapies, to be let in the back door and rarely addressed up front. They are often a trouble to be regulated, managed, or meditated away. You will harness the enormous energy and direction of emotions and easily integrate them into your profession or work life, without having to download a whole new school of psychotherapy.

This book is also for the curious, thoughtful and aware person who wants to bring emotional fulfillment for him or herself, children, family, and perhaps into all his/her relations. You want to know how emotions work, what purpose they serve, and how to put your emotions on your side. You may find it easy to intuitively agree with what you find in this book, and in a sense to find you knew it all along. Hopefully, you will take up the book and run with it.

For all, the book may seem like wholly new ground, simply because the wide world of emotions is never addressed by your schools, your family, your training, or even your best friends. You have had to pick up the learning as you go along, which is often piecemeal and sometimes contradictory. Now you have a chance to make sense of the whole of your emotional life and have it work for you.

For the more curious, the Emotional Fulfillment Series of Ebooks offers a concise, action-oriented self-help guides for fulfillment of each emotion. Those on **Anger, Loneliness** and **Shyness** are available now. All are based on the much larger book, **Emotional Fulfillment,** which has a chapter on each of the 14 basic emotions and over 400 citations. This will be published soon.

Chapter 1: Your world of emotions

The experience of emotions

Your world of emotions is so vast and varied that to find purpose in each emotion, it is helpful to sort out how you experience emotions in everyday life. This introduces the order of your own experience into your considerations and helps you define the bounds of emotions. Simple reflection on your own experience of emotion will surprise you and make you wonder and wish for understanding.

To begin with, emotions just happen and they happen all the time. They are as inevitable as gravity. We can have emotions about anything, from paper clips to pets. Emotions provide us energy to act, even though it may not be clear how to act.

We feel emotions in our body, not our head. We feel like we are inside them and that they come over us. The feelings are rarely as sharp and well located in our body as anger or fear can be at times. They are vaguely described as a choking, tightness, shakiness, flushing, or a knot in the belly. We may hardly notice them as they pass, and then we are calm again.

Emotions feel personal, like they belong to us, as few other experiences do. We learn to trust them to tell us where we stand on some event. Other persons can have very different feelings about the same thing, but we sense our emotions come from us and that they are true to us.

Emotions happen fast and can be experienced within one or two seconds of an event. This speed can be measured by changes in heart rate, skin conductance and many other bodily changes. When they are experienced quickly, they appear to be attached to specific words or events; they are more useful then. Sometimes, more time is required, along with more facts, for emotions to emerge. Emotions can be hard to sort out.

Emotions can also last a very long time, for years, if they are not resolved. These emotional states are sometimes called moods and, while some are benign, some cause us a lot of trouble. Moods such as loneliness, bitterness or depression, can color everything we do and make our attitudes and actions inflexible. Moods are a filter to our experience and make us pay attention to certain things in specific ways.

Emotions often come mixed, and require sorting out to be useful. We can look at an event in several ways and find fear, hurt, anger and more, for example. When we size up events, we find different consequences, and each with its own feeling. Sometimes emotions are habitually blended and become a blended set of feelings, like "guilt" or "disappointment." We have many names for such blends.

Our emotions continually respond to the changing circumstances of our life, in fact, most anything we experience. It would be difficult to reconstruct all the shifting feelings we experience in a single day, as one slides readily into the next At the same time, we are making decisions and taking action, drawing from our feelings. We may not be conscious of all of the emotions, as they seamlessly enter into our planning and rationalizing.

We have learned in a casual way to read and name our emotions as they enter into and guide our actions. We recognize the individual qualities and patterns to our bodily sensations, which give us an immediate sense of which emotion is afoot. Even though everyone's pattern of body sensations is a bit different, we can become familiar enough with our own that, if pressed, we can give the emotion a name.

Emotions have Purpose

In all, emotions are like an internal weather report that tells you how a situation affects you in vital ways. We have emotions about ourselves, too, that tell us how we are doing in life. We usually don't feel so keenly about situations that don't matter to us. Your weather report tells you which way the wind is blowing: what you need to do next, what you are in the mood for, the emotional consequences of your decision, and so on.

The purpose of this book is to learn about the essential purpose of each emotion and what fulfills it. The effect of an emotion on your life depends on what you do with it, that is, whether it is fulfilling or a source of stress and misery. When we act on each emotion to fulfill its purpose, the emotion fades, having served its purpose, no longer to goad or upset us. Doing this promotes balance and emotional maturity. When our needs, so often expressed through emotions, are met this way we experience peacefulness within ourselves. Applied to families, groups and nations, we can find peace in the world.

Myths about emotion

As much as we may recognize the truth of our perceptions in the last section, commonly held opinions about emotions blur and confuse us in ways that do harm to us.

One position is that emotions are <u>useless.</u> They belong to a primitive stage in human development when we had to react quickly, instinctively. Emotions don't help to digest information or make complicated decisions. More formally, the view is that emotions are dysfunctional and impair the logical, evidence-based decision-making that is part of man's unique rationality.

This position avoids the fact that emotions can guide and direct you beneath your awareness. It ungraciously ignores the zest and meaning that the positive emotions give to life. An impoverished emotional life leads to the stunted relations and barren inner life of a hermit or recluse. Neurological findings have established that emotions are actually essential to making and carrying out decisions.

Another is that emotions are upsetting and <u>dangerous </u>beasts that have to be tamed, i.e. the dark and chaotic Id. Each age has created its own vampires, witches, zombies, aliens and devils. Certainly, emotions can make one kill, torture or harm. This position leads to constant monitoring and a whole array of measures to control or suppress emotions. Projection is a defense that attributes your emotions to another person, thereby disowning them. Continual vigilance is the order of the day.

This position ignores the dynamic that the more you repress feelings, the more dangerous and intrusive they feel. That is because they persist in some form, regardless. Repressed anger can become complaining, complaining become resentment, and when you have made your case airtight, bitterness lies at the end. By fiercely de-emotionalizing life, you feed the dangerous beast, not tame it.

Another myth is that emotion is just an effect, an ornament not to be taken too seriously. In this case, emotions don't tell you much, except how well or ill things have turned out. A more extreme view is that emotions are crazy; they upset you and lead you astray. Better to ignore them as best as you can! They certainly cannot be taken as the basis of planning or initiating things.

This breezy disregard fails to make use of the richness of emotional life. It turns cause and effect on its head, neglecting to see that acting wisely on your feelings makes events turn out better. And it is very useful to know how events have turned out as measured by our feelings about them.

Another myth is that emotions cloud judgment and thought and lead to real trouble. The heat of the moment, the inflexible emotional position, the old hurt feeling – these make us act in ways to bring harm we can't take back easily. Right?

Of course, emotions that are acted on in ways to defend or attack get us into trouble, as with instinctive acts, the nurturing of negative emotions, or old protective habits. However, if emotions are acted on in fulfilling ways, ways that fulfill the essential purpose of each emotion, we will act in ways that complete the emotion and enable it to loosen its hold. Then, our judgment is better than ever.

Another myth is that emotions are <u>positive or negative</u>, as if each kind must lead us to a good or bad outcome. Certainly anger sounds negative, and has unpleasant bodily feelings. We may associate it with the most upsetting, harmful times of our lives. Yet anger can also keep us focused and determined to get something essential for us. It makes no sense that "negative" emotions have no purpose except to defeat us and make us feel bad.

A widely prevailing myth is that by simply labeling and <u>expressing</u> the emotion, you have then accepted it and are then in control. Eastern faiths view letting-go and non-action as necessary to spirituality. Meditation seminars of all types induce relaxation to banish the disruptiveness of emotions. Seminars train professionals to help others express and label feelings yet neglect what they should do about them, e.g. "get it out, tell us how you feel, and you'll feel better."

Despite its short-term effectiveness and the adept who can detach throughout the day, this view rides roughshod over the evidence of how useful and persistent emotions can be until they are resolved. In the lives of victims of trauma, abuse or neglect, powerful emotions can persist for many years, or a lifetime. They can motivate cruelty or kindness, ambition or humility, recklessness or protectiveness – all depending on how they are handled. Expression of emotion is only the beginning of the integration of emotion.

Setting it straight

Exposing these myths is only a start to untangling the misuse of emotions. The misuse – and abuse – of our emotional life is so rampant and varied, it requires the whole of this book to discriminate and identify the harmful and beneficial use of emotions. Here are some more entanglements:

> Losing yourself in an emotion, becoming it
> Displaying emotions for effect
> Addiction to one kind of emotional experience
> Emotional moods that persist for days, weeks, and longer

Sheer impulse release, damn the consequences
Abusing the power and control of emotions
Manipulating the feelings of others, without feeling for them
Emotional traps in our closest relations

The Chapters that Follow

The following chapters reveal the astonishing pathways of your emotions over a lifetime. First, I will present a brief story of emotions down through history. Then I will summarize the basic findings of science about emotions, followed by my Model for the development of all emotions. I will also show how each emotion plays a central role in our personal life, our family and community life, and even our national life. Throughout, I will expand on how the integration of your emotions can energize and enlighten education, health, morality, and even our whole world order.

My aim is no less than to restore this neglected, even demonized, area of human experience to its essential and central place in human nature. The following chapters will show how anger, as one of the major emotions, can either be fulfilling and freeing, or lead to self-defeat and misery. You will see how attempts to avoid, dominate or passively submit to anger can lead to a loss of your Selfhood, and lead to even the worst atrocities. The energy and direction of each emotion cannot be denied and can persist over a lifetime, recognized or not. When fulfilled, the emotion is transcended, you are free and you are blessed with a virtue.

While this is not a self-help book, it is a clear, down-to earth explanation of the purpose of your emotions and how they can be liberating and fulfilling. I'll be with you every step of the way.

Chapter 2: Emotions through History

As you saw in Chapter 1, myths about emotions abound in our time. In history, too, emotions make up a strained and muddled region of thought. In this chapter, I will present a short story of how we have looked at emotions through the ages. You will find growing acceptance and clarity. Now, in our time, the role of emotions in our life has become a central focus in understanding ourselves and what to do with them.

Philosophers and the Emotions

Emotions were a stepchild of the early philosophers. Their thinking was captured with the coming of written literature over 2500 years ago. For Socrates, emotions were bestial, less intelligent and dangerous, and for many others emotions were a form of disturbed judgment. Aristotle analyzed some common emotions in their components – bodily arousal, behavior, beliefs, and social norms – but he was more concerned with Ethics. The early Stoic philosophers were even more severe: emotions were poor judgments that led to misery (Oatley, 2004). The best life was "apatheia," or detachment from emotions. The Manual of Epictetus says "it is feelings that torment us, rather than the things themselves." Warning against envy, sadness, hurt, arrogance, and all forms of desire, he said that true freedom is "zestfully performing our duties." The Epicureans found pleasure important, but only in things that are natural and necessary, i.e. simple.

Chrysippus, a Greek Stoic, believed the first "movement" of an emotion is involuntary and reflexive (instinctive) and the second movement is more considered (reflective) and helps us decide what to do about the emotion (Sorabji, 2000). Later on, an early Christian, Lactantius, proposed not to eliminate emotions but that emotions "are planted in us by nature and have a purpose" and their value for good or bad depends on how they are used (Konstan, 2001). These two views are basic to the model for emotional development presented later in Chapter 4.

The Stoics had an enduring influence in the middle ages (and on some modern philosophers) but in this period emotions were linked to desires, especially selfish ones, under the influence of Christian theology. Greed, gluttony, lust, anger, envy, pride and sloth were the seven deadly sins as revised by Pope Gregory in the 6th century. The virtues of hope, faith, love and charity were not seen as emotions. Not until the 13th century were the seven heavenly virtues proposed as a form of remedy: chastity, abstinence, liberality, diligence, patience, kindness, and humility (Oatley, 2004).

In the 17th century, with the coming of the Enlightment, Descartes spurned the ancients, proclaiming that mind and body were separate "substances" and that reason could turn emotions into a good. Some "primitive passions" were even ingredients for the good life; passions such as wonder, love, hatred, desire, joy and sadness. In a similar way, Spinoza saw emotions as misguided judgments about the world, but that "active emotions" could bring us nearer to Divinity and bliss, and to our true nature. While Hume put a premium on science and rationality, he also saw some emotions as good, others as bad, but all being a motivation for morality. The moral sentiments, like sympathy, were the bedrock of society.

Beginning with Nietzsche and Romantics in the 19th century, passions became more central and even celebrated by philosophers like Rousseau. Some passions were wise, but others like resentment were clever, devious and disastrous. Nietzsche's dark picture of instinctive chaos appeared to have frightened other thinkers, and with the destructiveness of World War I, reason again ruled in philosophy.

The Emergence of Science

In America, questions about emotions were shuttled to the emerging science of psychology. James (1902, 1890) saw emotions as emerging from the action taken from them, or from the impulse to act in a certain way, explaining, "every object that excites an instinct excites an emotion as well." In Europe, thinkers tried to give emotions a more central place in life. Heidegger (2010) and Recouer defended emotions and moods as the way we tune into the world and form moral decisions. But, until the 1960's, emotions were slighted in research and the role of behavior and learning dominated research that was based largely on animal studies. Personal experiences of emotions were dismissed as "introspection" and not amenable to science. Since then, scientists and psychologists have collaborated with other disciplines to form a more inclusive view of emotions. Only recently has the self-preservative role of emotions expanded to include the "prosocial" emotions of compassion, altruism and belonging.

In the early 20th century psychotherapy literature, Freud (1930) conceived of some desires as unconscious, and that simply bringing them to consciousness will make us responsible for them. Beck (1974) thought the real villains were the automatic thoughts that instigate bad moods, such as anxiety and depression and that therapy helped you move to more realistic, constructive thoughts. More recently, emphasis has been on becoming aware of emotions, labeling them, detaching from them and managing them. However, "managing emotions" has taken the form of suppressing emotions, distracting from them, substituting positive attitudes, or opposing one emotion with another. Few have proposed understanding the true purpose of each emotion and how to fulfill it, so that the emotion is completed and loses its hold on you.

Even though our poetry and literature is rich with stories of basic emotions, we only recently have come to the brink of looking at emotions from many perspectives. In the next chapter, I will briefly summarize recent findings of both researchers and clinicians, so that you can see what emotions are made of, how they work and their importance to you. After that chapter, I will lay out my Model for Emotional Fulfillment, bringing all the evidence together, as well as my lifelong experience of working with the emotions of my clients.

Chapter 3: The Science of Emotions

In this chapter I will give you an essential idea of the research findings about emotions that have gathered over the last 50-60 years. Recently, there has been growing inquiry into bodily changes, brain mechanisms, and the biology of emotions. The causes of emotions are also now studied: the immediate situation, inherited predisposition, the individual's view, early

training, and the role of desires, culture, and many other influences. Even then, these studies have been uneven, often narrow, and there are few long-term studies about how emotions change over a lifetime.

The Feeling of an Emotion

The feeling of an emotion, so obvious to all, is still a stumbling block to science. One problem is subjectivity: is your "redness" my "redness"? Another is the enormous vocabulary for emotions, thousands of words that overlap, mix, and suggest the feeling of an emotion. Another is the lack of a measuring stick for an emotion, with numbers on it.

But D'Amazio (2003) and many others agree that the feeling of an emotion is what we experience in our body (i.e. a tight throat) as well as our perception of it. We perceive our body feeling through memories, associations, images, and end up with "I felt like going home." It is even a mystery how feelings become conscious. Panksepp (1998) feels consciousness evolved as a way of seeing the relevance of body feelings. Animals probably do not have the rich associations we do with our bodily feelings. The upshot is that while we sometimes don't agree on what emotion is being signaled by our body, we do fairly well, even across different cultures (Brown, 1991).

The feeling of an emotion changes as we grow up. In the first years, awareness of emotion is inward and reflexive. By ages 3-5, emotion combines a feeling in the body with an appraisal of the situation, and we can empathize with others. Later on, we can experience a blend of feelings and have complex responses to feelings. Adults can make distinctions, use accurate empathy, anticipate feelings and reflect on how they handle feelings. Shaver, P. et al (1992) feel that much of how we experience emotions is acquired by social and cultural learning.

Empathy

Most theorize that empathy for others develops at the pace with your awareness of your own emotional experiences. The evidence is that we experience another's feelings by a direct, swift "mapping," particularly for another's body feelings (Decety & Ickes, 2009). The same areas of our brain are active both when seeing someone in a situation and when being the situation ourselves. Surprisingly, the evidence is that empathy for others can occur within the first year of life in this automatic way.

Taking the perspective of another is part of empathy that develops much later (Nickerson et al, 2009), as it requires that we put ourselves imaginatively in the situation of the other person. Most animals can't do this. We draw on all of our experience – memories, images, stories, role-playing, etc. – to do this. Putting yourself in another's shoes is a creative construction.

The Biology of Emotions

We share with all warm-blooded animals the same emotions originating in the lower 1/3 of the brain, the reptilian brain (Panksepp, 1998). In humans, the experience of emotions is expanded in the mid-brain areas, which link the cingulate, the limbic system and mid-brain sensorimotor circuits to higher frontal and temporal areas of the brain. The higher 1/3 of the brain, the cortical areas, regulates, heightens or extends emotional feelings, through memory, imagination, foresight, judgment and language, among other abilities. In humans, these neural connections make emotions persist and influence us over long periods of time.

When neuroscientists have looked for patterns for a specific emotion in brain activity by MRI, etc., they find fairly regular patterns. In looking for patterns in bodily indicators like muscle tension, heat racing posture, etc., they also match up fairly well with common emotions like fear, anger and sadness. However, there has been no perfect matching either for the emotion of one person over time or between persons (Davis, 1994).

Instinct

The working definition of an instinct is a biologically-based series of actions that are automatic, inherited and coordinated (Damazio, 1994). Such emotions are triggered by a specific situation and promote survival and well-being. They are acted out in the same way by all members of the same species of animals. They appear early in life and are readily shaped and changed. For example, in fear, we instinctively freeze or take cover (McDougall, 1923).

Instinct has gone in and out of fashion ever since it was proposed in the 16th century (Maslow, 1997). Critics find it hard to tell the difference between instinctive and intelligent activities and complain that it is never fixed, but highly modified by your experience. To them, instinct seems "pure" only in its first performance, so the term has fallen into disuse.

In my model, instinct is essential in describing the initial, unreflective experience and acting-out of an emotion that can lead to all sorts of self-defeat and trouble. I will bring instinct into the Model for Emotional Fulfillment later on.

Basic Emotions

Most would agree that "basic" emotions are those not easily divided into more elementary parts and those that are inherited by all of a species (Oakley et al, 2006). Many theorists propose eight basic emotions (Tomkins, 1962; Izard, 1992). A more inclusive list has 14 basic emotions: fear, anger, sadness, disgust, hurt, envy, jealousy, insecurity, humor, wonder, joy, compassion, awe, and love (Roseman, 1984). Many terms for emotions mix several basic emotions at once. For example, guilt mixes disgust (an offensive deed), fear (of punishment), anger (at accusations), hurt (damage to your reputation), among others. Other terms can refer to a mindset years in the making, with many implied attitudes and beliefs, such as pride or shame. These terms for emotions are not so basic, however commonly used.

A basic emotion starts with a quick appraisal of a situation, bringing distinct bodily changes and an impulse to act in a certain way, all based on an inherited sensitivity and impulse (Izard, 1986). The basic emotion is triggered by typical situations, e.g. fear, when you are threatened. The action you do take is modified by your experience, memory, judgment, foresight and many other forms of thought.

The Causes of an Emotion

The immediate cause of an emotion is your relation to something or someone you care about (Lazarus, 1991). If the relation is"I've lost it forever," the emotion is sadness. You can have feelings about anything you care about, but rarely about things of no concern to you. Most investigators agree (Oakley & Johnson-Laird, 1987) that the awareness of the emotion and its meaning (its relation to something) arise almost simultaneously.

A contributing cause of an emotion is the circumstance that sharpens or heightens the relation you have. In the relation of fear of someone, threat is heightened by someone talking louder or moving closer. Persistent stress of everyday life can intensify your emotional response.

Emotions have predisposing causes as well. Your previous experience, your sensitivity, and your personality can all predispose you to feel one way or another. Trauma, childhood relations, and critical events are known to have a lifelong influence on what you feel (Young & Klosko, 1994). You can have well-developed emotions to very little stimulation, or cause, and without much reflection on its meaning. Someone's shout can feel that it was meant for you.

The purposeful cause of emotions is the reason for having that emotion in the first place, i.e. the evolutionary inheritance. However, the instinctive or Darwinian purpose, survival of the species, does not embrace the rich and varying flow of human emotions and experience. To Maslow (1997), the purpose of emotions is to fulfill a unique, human purpose, which is to enable growth of Self by completing the emotion and being free of it This can transform the emotion into a personal virtue. For example, by being prepared for a fear and facing up to it, we are freed from life-altering fear and acquire Courage. You will see more of this later in the next chapter.

Appraisal in Emotions

The relation you have to the event, i.e. its meaning, determines what emotion you feel. Lazarus (1991) first proposed that there is a relational meaning for each emotion. If someone frustrates an essential need, you will feel angry. While instinct gives you an automatic, quick appraisal, your reflection on the event just as quickly alters its meaning. What need is involved? What can you expect? How to cope? Where can you get help? Interestingly, too, the action you take can change your relation to the person or situation, and its meaning to you. The beliefs of your family or community can change your appraisal of the event, too. The role of appraisal in giving meaning to an emotion is now widely accepted.

The Urge to Act

Emotions contain tremendous energy to act at once. Early in emotion research, emotions were seen as a state of activation, which was not only a heightened arousal but a more vivid emotional feeling (Berlyne, 1960). This early research emphasized the energy in emotion, but not its direction.

Now this urge to act is seen as an attempt to maintain or change your relation to something you care about, i.e. protect, acquire, explore, enjoy, etc. Each emotion has a distinctive call for action (Izard, 1986). While instinctively the action may be automatic and unguided, for humans the emotion can begin reflection that changes the action in complex and purposeful ways.

Mood as Sustained Emotion

Mood is a long-lasting emotional state that is hard to shake off. Often the cause is not obvious, and it can be a long-established habit. The upshot is that you attribute the cause of the emotion to the situation you are in, no matter how relevant the situation is to our feeling. In a grumpy mood, nothing ever works out well. You will act according to your mood, and resist explanations that do not fit your mood. One study showed that those stuck in an anxious mood did not lower their estimate of risk even when given reassurance, while those temporarily anxious did. Forgas & Bower (1987) found that your mood especially affects you more when serious personal issues are at stake or when situations are unfamiliar or complex. Isen (1987) found that a positive mood increased flexibility in thinking, seeing relationships and creativity.

Unfortunately, research has focused much more on anxious or depressed moods, or on moods that last no more than a few hours, while neglecting moods associated with hurt, loneliness, shyness, anger, and other emotions. Questions remain about what makes a mood persist or stop. The larger purpose of moods and emotions in general has been neglected. I will clarify more about moods in Chapter 5, Moods and Entrapment.

Chapter 4: The Purpose of Emotion

An overview of what we know

An overview of the research and clinical writings in Chapter 3 is needed to provide the large canvas for this chapter on the purpose of emotions. I will include my own clinical experience in this summary, to further enlarge this overview.

To begin with, emotions just happen all the time, as part of our human nature. It's possible to have feelings about anything. They are a form of pure energy that can persist, remarkably, over a lifetime. There is usually a characteristic triggering event for each emotion with an immediate impulse to act in a certain way. Emotions tell us quickly our position towards this event, generally whether it is good for us or not. Emotions are unusually persistent and do not have to be conscious to affect our thoughts, decisions and actions. We are anatomically wired for emotions through the autonomic nervous system, brain anatomy, neuropeptides, and the instinctual system. Each primary emotion can be sensed and labeled fairly reliably by individuals. Each emotion often blends with other emotions, and we can even have emotions about emotions.

The benefit or cost of an emotion to us depends on how we act on it. Emotions not handled well become stress, which brings less energy, less health, more upset, and less capacity to respond positively. Over time, if emotions are not integrated into our life, they become trapped in rigid moods. Moods involve emotions in a tangle of thoughts, beliefs, attitudes, and action tendencies, a stuck way of looking at the world that does not allow completion of the feeling. The instinctive path of handling emotions leads to defensiveness and ultimately to rigid, stuck moods.

However, the reflective, distinctly human path of handling emotions allows their acceptance, integration and ultimate fulfillment. Fulfillment of any emotion means its purpose has been filled, the emotion completed, and its disappearance. Emotional freedom is a sense of having relatively few unfulfilled emotional claims. All emotions originate with our loves and attachments, and our happiness is their fulfillment through constant contact, skill, and dedication. Peacefulness is a dynamic process of regular, dependable fulfillment of our emotional life.

Features of my Model for Emotional Fulfillment

Time

As a form of persistent, dynamic energy that ensures action, relatively little attention has been given to how emotions change over time. This reflects the expense and difficulty of research that takes years to unfold. Yet time itself gives us the opportunity to learn about and resolve our feelings. When we change our beliefs, appraisals, thoughts and actions in regard to a strong emotion, the experience of the emotion itself changes. In the Epilogue I relate how I came to appreciate this. In any case, one essential dimension of the model is time.

Choice

Another essential feature is the basic choice of acting on primary emotion either in an instinctual, impulsive way, or in a reflective, fully human way. As explained in Chapter 3, the instinctive choice is an inherited, relatively fixed way of responding to a life event in ways that seem designed for self-preservation and safety. I hope to show in this and later chapters how defensive, upsetting, destructive and ultimately self-defeating this path is, not only for individuals, but for community, the nations and international relations. The reflective choice – the authentic purpose of human emotions – leads to self-awareness, appreciation of one's feelings and circumstances, and ultimately to action that fulfills the emotion. When the purpose of an emotion is fulfilled, there is no more need for it, and it disappears. You are left with a sense of personal freedom and the opportunity for growth, not just protection.

Purpose

Another essential feature of the model is the purpose of emotions. This is not the adaptive role of emotions, a term that too loosely describes any function of emotion, such as emotional release, the communication value of emotion, the use of emotions for effect, etc. It is not the instrumental use of emotions to persuade, command or perform in a play, to someone's ulterior purpose. I mean the essential purpose like that of a river whose purpose is to drain the land and find the sea, while it may have many other functions and benefits. The human purpose of emotion is fulfillment of _Self,_ a uniquely human purpose that goes far beyond instinctual release. Fulfillment means a transformation of the emotion into a virtue and fulfilling your human potential. Who would not find a distinctly human purpose in emotions, which are so abundant, so inevitable, so responsive, so long-lasting, so much part of our decisions, and so much the flavor of our life? Seeing them as part of every animal endowment, and of a unique purpose for humans, restores them to the organizing and directing function they have, and to communality with all life.

The Model for Emotional Fulfillment

A diagram helps you see the relations between the elements of my model. At the risk of over-simplification, I present the Model below with the explanation following. In this diagram, the progression left to right occurs over time. This can be a matter of days or weeks, but with more complex events it may reflect years.

                                                    Entrapment
                                    Entanglement->
                            Alarm->
Trigger-> Basic emotion ->
                            Challenge->
                                    Integration->
                                                    Fulfillment

The instinctive pathway refers to a simple, automatic reflexive response that occurs without much awareness. It occurs quickly as an all or nothing emotional response; an alarm. It urges you to act in a specific way that is common to all animals and human beings. In the instinctive response, you become entangled in the feeling, by defending against it in a wide variety of ways: by avoiding the feeling, by submitting to it, or even adopting its power. The end result is being entrapped in a way of life that feeds the emotion, without resolving it.

The reflective pathway begins with awareness of the situation and appraisal of your needs. It presents a challenge. It then integrates emotion with thought, reasoning and action, and an ability to empathize objectively, anticipating the needs and feelings of others. Reflection can weigh the consequences of action, compare and contrast, recall similar events, make plans and choose a course of action. The end result is fulfillment of the emotion.

The model above is highly conceptual and can be better understood by applying it to a single basic emotion. Consider the outcome of **anger** over time, handled instinctively or reflectively:

Instinctive Pathway

                                          Entrapment
                                          Bitterness
                                          Victimhood
                    Entanglement->   Dominance
                    Blame   Disillusion
                    Attack   Hatred
    Alarm->   Retaliation
    Frustration   Resentment
    Impatient
    Strike back

Trigger-> **Emotion**->
A need is   Anger
frustrated

        Challenge->
        Acceptance
        Consideration
        Clarify need   **Integration**->
                         Assert need
                         Get help   **Fulfillment**
                         Options   Get needs met
                         Negotiate   Mastery
                                       Contentment

Fulfillment Pathway

The Stages of Anger in Each Pathway

The **triggering event** for anger is the perception of being blocked or turned away from an authentic need. It can be the bureaucrat's paperwork, a stolen parking space, the destruction of a house of worship, or the amorphous enemy of stop and go traffic. It can be as slight as a single mother's broken glass, if that is the last straw in a series of frustrations. The triggering event does not necessarily produce hurt, being fearful or saddened, although anger easily recruits these emotions secondarily, which makes for more entanglement.

The **emotion** itself is a primary emotion, one common to all animals, out of which humans create infinite blendings with other primary emotions. Anger, for example, blends with other emotions to form guilt, a tangled web of feelings. These can include fear (of being punished), hurt (at being judged), sadness (loss of stature), embarrassment (at exposure), disgust (with one's transgression), as well as anger itself (frustrated in filling a need). Anger and other primary emotions are further described in my same two-path model in later chapters, as well as the implications for the individual, community, and international relations.

Alarm or Challenge

Even at the earliest stage of awareness of feeling, the alarm/challenge stage, whether one begins the instinctive or reflective path can be a conscious choice. If the mind-set is internal, the beginning of introspection, you are aware of a need that is being overridden, and you think of it as a challenge. Being true to one's need, one focuses on that need and keeps track of it. The degree of anger reminds us of the intensity of that need. We have **a Challenge.**

If we focus on the barrier, our mindset is external and we experience anger as an **Alarm.** A need is blocked, pushed aside, ignored, delayed, forbidden, or ridiculed. Much of anger is then directed towards the one who frustrated us, or what was in the way, or what injustice was done, or the evilness of the frustrator, and much more. The focus immediately is the barrier, not the goal, i.e. the reasons why we cannot achieve our need, rather than how to fill it. This focus distorts our thinking, magnifying enormously the power of the frustrator, and often brings in naturally the emotions of fear and hurt. We want to act and not let this go by.

Entanglement or Integration

In mid-path, the **Entanglement** of emotional resolution, life gets complicated and troubled, owing to the power of the human mind to remember, conceptualize, create beliefs, judge, predict and more. Defenses generally take the form of avoiding, minimizing or identifying with the emotion. For example, whole lifestyles can be built around the defensive handling of anger: explosive tripwire anger, suppression, cold seething anger, martyred and victimized anger, sly passive-aggressive anger, vengeance and retribution, uninhibited hysterical anger, easy violence, and murderous rages. While the instinctive, entangled handling of anger feels powerful and controlling, you miss the whole purpose of anger: to fill an authentic need.

On the other hand, the reflective path attempts **integration**, recognizing the priorities of your needs. You look assertively for fulfillment, clarifying what would satisfy. This focus inward keeps you from the waste of blaming, resenting and excuse-making as these take you further and further from your goal. In anger, integration means looking for sources of help, asserting one's needs to appropriate people, looking for win-win compromises, negotiating in good faith, and forming plans. Oddly, the most difficult thing to say in the heat of anger is what would most satisfy your need.

Entrapment or Fulfillment

One last stage of the emotional resolution, the **Entrapment** stage, is a consequence of how one's anger was handled in the first two stages. Once your anger has hardened, the enemy has been demonized, and there has been little satisfaction of need. Bitterness sets in as a mood, a rigid way of viewing the world with rancor, old grudges, disillusionment, and vast discontent. You see this mood in older persons whose life has turned out, and now are cranks, grouches and soreheads, quick to take offense and complain. These moods can be so held in place by beliefs, habit and behavior, that even real satisfactions are refused or minimized. This is the ultimate in being trapped and self-defeated.

On the other hand, the **Fulfillment** pathway of handling anger ensures that one's needs are met, even if bit by bit and over time. In this process of integrating anger into one's life situation, by seeking help, studying alternatives, being assertive, and more, we acquire an acute sense of participation in what life has to offer and a sense of mastery in meeting one's needs. This state of mind is not so much a mood as a transcendence of emotion, a virtual transformation of raw anger into Fulfillment, such that the anger vanishes, and no longer exists as a sizzling, rampant bundle of energy. Chapter 6 will explore this transformation as something akin to spiritual energy or virtue and discusses its implications for the individual and community.

An abbreviated table for the development and purpose of all the major emotions.

The table below summarizes my longer, well-documented book that is based on psychological science and many other disciplines, as well as my direct clinical experience. It will be published soon. There are over 400 references. Each emotion has a separate chapter, with commentary on the implications of emotional fulfillment for families, communities, and the nations. There are additional chapters on Education, Morality and Psychotherapy.

Emotion	Relation	Purpose	Fulfillment	Virtue	Entrapment
Fear	Threat	Face up	Freedom	Courage	Oppression
Anger	Frustrated	Assertion	Satisfied	Contentment	Bitterness
Sadness	Loss	Reflection	Renewal	Faith	Hopeless
Lonely	Unloved	Reveal self	Genuine	Authenticity	Fakeness
Shyness	Separate	Play a role	Belong	Member	Alienated
Hurt	Damaged	Heal self	Reconcile	Forgive	Withdrawal
Envy	Left out	Value	Appreciate	Gratitude	Greed
Disgust	Tainted	Evaluate	Respect	Charity	Contempt
Awe	Inspired	Whole	Transform	Spirituality	Lessened
Insecure	Depend	Self-care	Assurance	Independent	Incompetent
Jealousy	Stolen	Affirm	Commit	Charity	Uncertainty
Love	Identify	Engage	Joy	Compassion	Emptyiness
Humor	Absurd	Release	Lightened	Acceptence	Heaviness
Curiosity	Intriguing	Explore	Understand	Open-minded	Close-minded

An explanation of the terms in the abbreviated table

Emotion is one of the 14 basic emotions most agree to. Many more are combinations of emotions or refer to a certain time and circumstance. Relation refers to your emotional relation to what you value, e.g. if what you value is threatened, you feel fear. What you value can be anything: yourself, others, things or values themselves.
Purpose refers to the uniquely human action you take to fulfill the emotion, different from all warm-blooded animals. These simple words refer to mature responsibilities and need much more explanation.
Fulfillment of the emotion describes the end-result of integrating the emotion into your life, and using its energy and direction to complete the emotions, and be free of it. It is a transformation.
Virtue is the outcome of the emotion if it is handled in a fulfilling way; a way of being in the world that honors all living beings, and a way that becomes part of one's character.
Entrapment is the outcome of handling an emotion instinctively and impulsively, which can involve submitting to the emotion, defending against it, or even identifying with the emotion. The outcome of Entrapment is the opposite of the outcome of Fulfillment.

Next: a closer look.

The next two chapters will take a close look at the two different outcomes in handling emotion: Entrapment or Fulfillment. Chapter 5 will clarify how Entrapment can take the form of a persistent, self-defeating mood, or way of life, and even a personality disorder. Our experience of mood, some basic research, a good look at depression, and my model for moods and their destructiveness will be explained. In Chapter 6, you will see how Fulfillment is experienced, with selected views on happiness and related research. The centrality of love will then be discussed and the hope that fulfillment offers you, your family and community.

Chapter 5: Moods and Entrapment

Overview

We all feel we know what moods are, what it is to be moody, what we are in the mood for, and so on. And yet mood is a word that splashes around several meanings. In psychological research moods are seen as conceptually and operationally unclear (Frija, 1986). Most clinical literature is narrowly confined to depression, mania and anxious moods. Much more expression of moods is found in music, movies and everyday experience.

For this chapter, after describing how we experience moods, I will outline the research on moods. Then my Model for moods will show how they are the end result of acting instinctively on your emotions, ending in Entrapment. I will describe with many examples how entrapping moods are, including how destructive they are, to your sense of Self and to others. I will also propose how moods can be hardened into fixed ways of life called personality disorders and the primary emotions in each.

The Experience of Moods

Emotions are like going down a river: we make choices as we take the ride. Moods are like being stuck in a swamp, going nowhere, with not much choice at all.

Moods seem to come with their own story line, and even a cast of characters, staging and lighting. Whatever happens around you is interpreted in the light of the mood.

The story can be "I am lonely and unloved," and the characters wander, footsteps echo, and distance grows. All characters move as unreal as ghosts. When will my life begin? Or the story may be "I'm bitter and disillusioned," and then everything seems pointless, everyone gets in each other's' way, or just seem annoying. Nothing ever turns out right. The staging is rickety, draped from disuse, and dusty. If the mood is

"People are contemptible and beneath me," people seem to have empty roles and mock themselves. They keep each other at arm's length and their music is like tin whistles, thin and cheap.

Moods determine how we act, just as surely as if we were costumed, staged and rehearsed. It feels like the only way to act. Others will see this mood on our face, our movements, our voice and what we do. For example, if we are depressed, the story is "There is no hope left for me" and we slow down and sag, our thoughts are pushed, and it feels hard to start anything. Our voice is flat, our face stiff. We are stuck in a sad role and can't get back.

We can get so lost in a mood it becomes a way of life. Over time, we can even find comfort in it, get ways to justify it, and develop fixed beliefs about it. For example, if you have lived a non-social life, with few commitments to others, you may embrace a mood of alienation. The world has little to offer you and you reject it. You may join a group of alienated persons who can share their separateness. More extreme, you may form a belief in a radical cause, to find the security of a true believer or to find redemption.

It takes time to recognize our moods as they move in and out of our lives. But, in time, we recognize some are "regulars"and we see how they make us feel and act. If our mood is shame, we know we will comfort ourselves by being alone, and try to do something constructive. We will protect ourselves by disappearing into the work of routines. We construct beliefs about how we have been wronged. In all this, we unwittingly construct the space for our mood to return more easily and create a guilty way of life.

The Research on Moods

In my model, moods are another term for the end-result of the instinctive path: entanglement and entrapment of a basic emotion. I offer this summary of the research bearing on this last stage of emotional entrapment, or mood.

Distinction: Emotion vs. Mood

Most scientists agree on the distinction between emotion and mood. Emotions are more likely to be reactions to specific situations, while moods originate in the sensitivities inside you, and are projected onto the situation you are in (Forgas, 1993). Emotions last for a relatively short time, an average of 8 minutes or so for some investigators (Ekman, 1994). Moods last much longer, for hours in just one event or over years, by being repeated over and over (Watson & Clark, 1994). Much of the study of moods have used a short-term induction of a mood and often in a situation of limited emotional intensity, so it is difficult to find studies of moods lasting months or years, other than moods of depression or anxiety.

Triggers for Moods

While mood seems to be caused by the situation you are in, your sensitivity to unresolved emotion is a much more likely trigger (Lazarus, 1999). You are all too ready to feel your unresolved, habitual emotion contained in the mood. The returning veteran who has lived with unremitting, traumatic danger finds that any sudden, unexpected sound or move can trigger overwhelming fear of present danger (Meichenbaum, 1994). This trigger can also come from early childhood relations with your caregiver, from situations of shaming/disgust, abandonment/loneliness, social rejection/shyness, physical or emotional abuse/fear, and others (Young & Klosko, 1994). Any occasion of great hurt, if unresolved, can easily form a sensitivity that needs little reminder to cause alarm and reinstate the emotions that go with it, e.g. hurt, fear, distrust, anger and others. All emotions, if intense and unresolved, can bring on a mood so intense it may feel like you are reliving the original situation.

Early development of mood

Early care giving and trauma before the age of five can form the most persistent moods, or entrapments. Young & Klasko (1994) have identified 18 parental (caregiver) relations that form "lifetraps." By entering and distorting all key relations later on in life, they are unusually persistent and influential. For example, in the emotional deprivation lifetrap, you have been neglected and not given attention and nurturance early in life. Later on, in romantic or key relations, you feel loneliness as a major emotion, and feel disconnected and empty. Each "lifetrap" is a pattern of beliefs, attitudes, expectations and emotions that has hardened into a way of life that seems natural to you. Each lifetrap is driven by a major emotion, or combination of emotions, that is rarely fulfilled.

Beliefs and Mood

The more you ruminate and brood on your mood, the more fixed are your beliefs about the causes of the mood. Frija & Mesquita (2000) feel that the emotion in mood makes for selective attention which, in turn, provides information that strengthens the belief. These beliefs then can cause more upset feelings, which returns you to more brooding – a vicious circle. Brooding rehearses these events and feelings about them so that your beliefs become more and more fixed and unlikely to change. This prevents a reappraisal of the situation that might lead to positive change. Ultimately, even new events unrelated to the trigger event are often interpreted in the light of the mood. The persistence of moods is seen in one study when 70% of those who were relieved of depressive symptoms by antidepressants found a return of depressive mood once medication was stopped.

Judgment and Mood

Judgment is directly affected by your mood, particularly where you lack much personal investment in the outcome, or when you are unable to think clearly The more you are told to pay attention to your mood, the more your judgment is affected by mood (Forgas, 1993). In one study, by just having a person write about a recent happy or sad event, then events occurring right after the writing are interpreted in the light of that mood. But where judges are "well-rehearsed" or have a highly motivated strategy, they were less swayed by mood (Frija &Vargas,

2004). A positive mood helps flexibility in thinking, and in seeing relationships, all of which help creativity (Isen, 1987)

The Physiology of Mood

Mood, or a lasting emotional outlook, can cause physiological changes in your body. For example, Kaga, Reynick and Suidian (1988) found that shy children had increased heart rate, larger pupil dilation, laryngeal muscle tension and more norepinephrine. Unresolved emotions, or stress, can contribute to the onset of diseases such as cancer, coronary heart disease, infectious diseases and poor wound healing (Leventhal & Patrick-Miller, 2003). Negative moods, too, have been shown to affect immune function adversely, and contribute generally to poorer health (Zautra, 2003).

Studies on the physiology of emotions show that while it is hard to discriminate between emotions on the basis of heart rate, brain activity, endocrine and immune systems, all emotions have effects on the body. Unfortunately, moods have not received as much attention.

Action Tendencies in Mood

According to Clore et al (1994), the narrow focus of emotion in a mood can lead to extreme belief and rash action. You lose all sense of proportion. In turn, acting on your mood can also confirm the beliefs you hold in that mood (Tesser et al, 1995). In a mood, you also are apt to remember events that evoke a similar mood, events that seem to back up your action. For example, childhood trauma can make brain changes that make for moodiness that impairs an accurate assessment of social situations (Thompson & Meyer, 2007). Such mood-based memories set up a drama, with roles that can be quickly acted out in public.

Comments on Research of Moods

Most attention in mood research has been given to moods relating to depression and anxiety, as they are most distinctly recognized in the psychiatric diagnostic manual, DSM IV. About 95% of clinical references are to these two, with anxious mood less often. Other moods which are as persistent and of great influence, such as those based on loneliness, boredom, shame, greed, bitterness, have got much less attention. In addition, research has focused more on emotions rather than moods, which are more difficult to study.

Depression Research

I present here an overview of the research on depression to give you a sense of the potential for research in refining and shaping what we know of mood. Hopefully other mood disorders than depression will get this attention, as well.

Clinical depression is diagnosed from the symptoms of an inner sense of worthlessness, fatigue, inability to concentrate, a loss of interest in usual pleasures, poor sleep, reduced or increased appetite and the loss of hopefulness. Those trapped in depression for years can get lost in sadness, withdraw from the world and increasingly yearn for the deceased to return. A major source of pain is not finding the loved one, over and over. The bereaved can lose track of who they are and what life means to them. Bonanno (2004) affirms that prolonged grief is most likely when you have had an emotional dependency on a loved one.

Bonanno (2004) followed the three most common grief reactions up to two years after the loss. About 30%, the majority called "resilient," coped effectively with their grief, moving through their pain and loss in a few weeks. Another 40% moved through extreme grief to recovery in a year or two. Another 10-15% had the same high levels of symptoms of grief at least two years after the loss (Bonanno & Field, 2001). These findings disagree with the early assumptions of psychoanalysts such as Freud, Deutch, and Lindemann that grief work is time-consuming and can be much delayed. Early theories of bereavement emphasized working through predictable and necessary stages until all ties were severed to the loved one (Kubler-Ross, 1973).

Most agree that the central emotion in grief is intense sadness at the loss of someone or something dear to you (Lazarus, 1991). Sadness makes you turn attention inward, be more detail-oriented and have more accurate judgments (Storbeck & Clore, 2005). This promotes deep reflection. The sadness in depression also dampens your physiology, such as heart rate and respiration, and makes you slow down (Werling, 2005). This gives the depressed person a "time-out" for reflection. Several authors have come to see this rumination is essential to take stock, review priorities, and renew hope.

Anger and contempt are emotions that are readily recruited in bereavement; emotions directed at yourself or the lost one. Humor occurs naturally in the resilient survivor of loss and appears to help with the loss (Bonanno & Keltner, 1997). More recent research has found that you get over grief more quickly by going between experiences of loss and experiences of hopefulness, two separate processes (Stroebe & Schut, 1999).

Resilience is fairly common in both children and adults (Christ, 2000). It does not depend upon whether the relations to the deceased one was really healthy or not, as most survivors idealize their lost loved one and recall the best of them (Bonanno, 2002). The resilient are less likely to use avoidance, distraction or diverting their attention as a way of softening the loss. They are more apt to be flexible in how they respond to the loss. Being more optimistic as well, they find more ways to move on (Alim et al, 2008).

The resilient also have more competence in how they express their emotions and in their social skills. Bonanno (2009) found that those who could flexibly switch between expressing and suppressing their emotions, whatever was necessary, did best. He feels "humans are wired for sadness" to help you "reflect on their loss, take stock and accept what cannot be undone " and then move on with life.

My Model for Moods

As you have seen in the tables and explanation in Chapter 4, Mood is another name for Entrapment, the end result of handling an emotion instinctively. This begins with instinctive Alarm over emotions and, over time, becomes an Entanglement in fixed beliefs and ways of handling your emotions. The end result is a trapped way of life, Entrapment.

Alarm and Entanglement

Alarm and entanglement are the first two stages in my model that can lead to rigid moods.

By **Alarm**, I mean your first notice of the feeling and your perception of a threat to your safety or someone/something dear to you. This focuses you on protective measures, which you can call defenses that further entangle you in the emotion. Instinctively, you focus on the external event that triggered the emotion. This focus keeps the emotion alive, unresolved and can lead to reckless, instinctive action.

There are three general types of **Entanglement** (Young et al, 2003). The first is when you try to soften or suppress the emotion by avoiding or minimizing the feeling. Distraction, displacement, denying, minimizing, projecting feelings onto someone else, ignoring feelings, are some of the more common ways. A second type of defense is to identify with the emotion and adopt it as your own. Instead of being the fearful or angry one, you become the intimidator or the bully. Another type of protection is to resign yourself to being intimidated (fear) or being bullied (anger) and become a victim or martyr instead. While these may seem weak measures to handle strong emotion, there are many readily available roles offered by our culture that actively entangle you in these ways. Entanglement keeps the emotion active by exciting you and urging action.

For example, in Anger development presented in Chapter 4, the three general types of entanglement are clear. In **minimizing** the feeling of anger, many stuff or deny it, or become very indirect about their own anger, i.e. passive aggressive gossip. Some will shrug it off and try to go on to the next thing. Still others will displace their anger onto some easy target, like the dog. By **identifying** with the emotion, some will become anger itself, and let anger enter all their relations. They will swagger, intimidate, accuse, threaten, bully and plan revenge. This easily can become a way of life as it offers control and dominance for those who have lived without them. **Resigning** yourself to the anger of others is to play the role of victim and draw pity, solace, and kindness from others. The martyr is skilled at compelling compassion with his/her account of cruelty or abuse of others.

My upcoming Ebooks show how the development of each of the 14 basic emotions leads to either Entrapment or Fulfillment.

A Mood for every emotion

My model expands the use of "Mood" to include all the basic emotions, not just those of fear (Anxious mood) or sadness (Depression). As you saw in Chapter 4, for every emotion there is a relation you have to someone/something you hold dear. You saw that if you go down the blind, instinctive path of handling that emotion, it leads to Entrapment of the emotion: a mood that becomes a way of life.

Emotion	Relation	Mood/Entrapment
Fear	Threat	Oppression
Anger	Frustration	Bitterness
Sadness	Loss	Depression
Loneliness	Unloved	Fakeness
Shyness	Separation	Alienation
Hurt	Damaged	Withdrawal
Envy	Needy	Greed
Disgust	Tainted	Contempt
Awe	Inspired	Insignificance
Insecurity	Dependence	Incompetence
Jealousy	Stolen	Abandonment
Love	Identify with	Emptiness

Humor	Absurd	Heaviness
Curiosity	Intriguing	Close-minded

These moods are widely recognized in our common experience, but rarely in research, and not often in the clinical literature. Each of these moods are clarified and expanded greatly in each book in the Emotional Fulfillment Series, which are self-help guides to avoiding these moods and finding Fulfillment instead.

Chapter 6: The Destructiveness of Moods

In this section I will look at the most harrowing aspects of moods, a descent into the heart of darkness. This is only to help you look down the road you may be on, and help you make choices, not to scare the daylights out of you. It is true that there are positive moods, but I feel that they may be better characterized as healthy moods, or just "virtues', since they are not rigid or entrapping and they do preserve your sense of Self and your personal freedom. Here are some of the ways that moods are not just self-defeating but destructive.

Moods freeze feelings, beliefs and action

In looking at the world through the filter of mood, we size up events as we feel inside. We confirm our beliefs about what we see thereby, as well as how we should act. Since the mood, action and beliefs can come on very quickly, it is easy to become committed to that action and no other. In anger, we may attack, retaliate, abuse and humiliate another and find it hard to take that back. Anger and isolation can lead to the planning and execution of mass killings. With the support of others, revenge can be not only an immediate act but also the reaction to centuries of wrongs and abuse, and the push behind warfare lasting for centuries. Justified war becomes an international principle that does not allow for neutrality. Our need to belong joins up with hurt and anger, and leads to the worst atrocities of war: rape, torture, pillage, and use of the most destructive forces available. No matter what the mood – greed, bitterness, alienation, and contempt – the effect of sharing it with others is to strengthen and confirm the underlying belief, the emotion, and the actions we have taken. We can lose our selves in the process.

Moods weaken our sense of Self

Because we are more limited in a mood that imposes and fixes action and belief, we cannot easily consider other alternatives. Even our memories, imagination, judgment and planning are bound and less useful to us. It is especially hard to consider an opposite to the way our mood dictates. For example, in shyness (the mood of alienation) we will do anything but reveal a damaging secret about ourselves. When in a prolonged mood, our Self in a sense is drowned out by the mood, and over time we can lose our awareness of our essential, true Self. Here are more examples of how our Self is weakened when in a prolonged mood:

> In a fearful mood, do anything but face up to the fearful thing
> In a sad mood, do anything but let go of the lost person or past
> In an affectionate mood, do anything but express your affection
> In a mood of hurt, do anything but forgive and get cared for
> In a jealous mood, do anything but give your loved one freedom
> In an envious mood, do anything but reflect on what you value
> In a lonely mood, do anything but reveal ourselves as we are

When we have lost our sense of Self, we cannot be ourselves. The tragedy of not being able to have a good relation with one's Self cannot be overestimated. For example, if you have not been able to be genuine with at least one intimate partner, loneliness condemns you to not only feeling fake but also feeling everyone around you is fake. You spend a lifetime inventing new fake characters for your persona, and living in horrifying fear that you will be found out, exposed as Fake. You feel less and less for everyone around you, including yourself.

Moods make you less responsible

Stuck in a mood, and not being able to consider alternatives, you are less able to look after someone or something you really care about. It's hard to consider alternatives, what information you need, the help you want, the results that will satisfy. At the same time, the basic emotion in each mood has a uniquely human purpose that cries for responsible action. The chart below shows what the core emotions are for various moods, as well as the responsible action that fulfills the emotion's purpose and frees you.

Mood	Basic emotion	Action needed	Fulfillment
Oppression	Fear	Face up to fear	Courage
Bitterness	Anger	Assert needs	Satisfaction
Hopelessness	Sadness	Reflection	Renewal of hope
Alienation	Shyness	Play role	Belonging
Withdrawal	Hurt	Healing for self	Forgiveness
Greed	Envy	Find true value	Gratitude
Contempt	Disgust	Evaluate wholly	Fairness
Insignificance	Awe	Embrace whole	Spirituality
Dependence	Insecurity	Care for self	Independence
Abandonment	Jealousy	Let go	Affirmation
Detachment	Love	Engage	Compassion
Heaviness	Humor	Enjoy incongruity	Lightened
Close-minded	Curiosity	Explore	Open-minded
Coldness	Empathy	See, feel for	Humanity

Moods dampen your empathy for others

The mood you are trapped in does not tolerate different points of view or the emotions that go with them. In the angry mood of bitterness and disillusionment, you do not feel for the strivings of others. You are more apt to feel contempt and to wish failure for their strivings. For all moods, you are less apt to tolerate humor, kindness, encouragement and compassion for the other's position, because your mood feels more real and essential. With little or no empathy, you become capable of needless hurt and even cruelty.

Personality Disorders and Moods

Personality disorders make up a diagnostic category in the DSM IV, the official diagnostic manual of the APA. They refer to 10 different patterns of relating to the world that are chronic, rigid and maladaptive. The most striking effect is to have relationships that are full of problems and hardships. They affect about 10% of adults (Torgensen, 2005).

Personality disorders illustrate how the effect of emotions has been neglected in the diagnosis, causes and treatment of these disorders In my view, each personality disorder can be called an entrapment, a rigid pattern of thinking of each disorder based on "problematic behaviors and traits" (Hoermann et al, 2011). But much less attention is given to the emotional aspects, even though two out of the four "traits" of these diagnoses are called "affectivity" and "impulse control." Even the new diagnostic manual (DSM V) bases the diagnoses on "dimensional" aspects of personality, i.e. dominance/submission. This approach likewise neglects the role of emotion. In general, an understanding of how emotions develop over time into fixed moods is neglected in most references to these diagnoses.

I wish to restore the centrality of emotions to personality disorders by showing how the entrapment of each emotion leads to a personality disorder. My model shows how the instinctive development of emotions over time becomes an entanglement and hardened mood, called a personality disorder. My model also helps explain how "co-occurring disorders," like a social phobia and an avoidant personality disorder can be diagnosed together. Both share fear and shyness as basic emotions and the model allows that the social phobia is more treatable as an Axis I disorder.

Of all this sounds increasingly technical, it is. This reflects the difficulties experts have in understanding personality disorders. Kupfer (2002) expressed a need to uncover the deeper underlying causes of personality disorders, and calls for a "yet unknown paradigm shift." The role of emotions in personality disorders may be that deeper influence. As Plutchik (2000) puts it, each emotion gives rise to a relationship pattern, or trait; and extreme traits are the basis of a personality disorder.

To clarify further, the following diagram shows the role of the basic and recruited emotions in each personality disorder, as I see it:

Personality Disorder	Basic Emotion	Recruited Emotions	Emotion-based Relationships
Paranoid .	Fear	Anger, Disgust	Hostility, Scorn, Defiance
Schizoid	Loneliness	Anger. Coldness	Fakeness, Frustration
Antisocial	Anger	Insecurity, Cold	Control, Dominance
Histrionic.	Belonging	Anger, Hurt	Exhibitionistic, Seductive
Narcissistic	Anger	Jealous, Insecure	Entitlement, Control
Borderline	Hurt	Anger, Disgust	Emotionality, Frustration
Avoidant .	Fear	Shyness, Depend	Threatened, Alienated
Dependent	Insecurity	Fear, Hurt	Helpless, Threatened
Ob-Comp	Fear	Disgust, Insecure	Threatened, Tainted

The ability of a single emotion to change over time, recruit other emotions, bring in habitual defenses, motivate behavior and morph into a way of life is central to the organization of what we call personality. In the end, each person with a rigid personality disorder can still have a great variety of emotional expression. When the major emotions are mixed with varying recruited emotions, a more complete understanding and a more complex picture emerges. Also, the defenses that seek to avoid, dominate or submit to each emotion make for a more complete picture of the personality disorder. It may be that any diagnostic formulation will never capture the variety within the diagnosis. Still, the emotions involved describe the essential relational problem and its influence on thinking and behavior for each personality disorder.

In the next chapter, we will see how the pursuit of happiness, or more simply, the pursuit of our loves, helps to transform and vanish the entanglements of our emotions. We will look more closely at the fulfilling outcomes of pursuing the reflective path of the emotions.

Chapter 7: The Promise of Emotional Fulfillment

This chapter may be as engaging for you to read as it was for me to write. To begin with, all the clinical and research literature has given much more attention to the troubles and upsets of emotions than the positive. And even then, there are many versions of fulfillment or happiness afloat, some contradicting others. And most of all, there is something elusive about Fulfillment itself, mainly because the emotional feelings of contentment, joy and even love are not as sharp and alerting as the most basic emotions like fear and anger. Tolstoy said, "Happy families are all alike" without saying just how. So, because my model speaks to the positive purpose of emotions, Fulfillment, I will put together my best evidence and experience to illuminate this uniquely human purpose of your emotional life.

This chapter begins with the experience of emotional fulfillment and then gives an overview of what fulfillment has meant to different authors. Then I will present a brief survey of the research findings about fulfillment. Then I will describe how Fulfillment is a true transformation of emotional experiences into what you can call "virtue" or "character," in which your sense of Self is affirmed. Also, I will show how the ultimate goal of fulfillment is Love, just as Love is the origin of all emotions. A following chapter will show how emotional fulfillment can benefit families and even nations, as well.

The experience of fulfillment

Haven't we all have had "peak experiences" in which everything enjoyable and good comes together and we wish it could happen again? We are heartened. It may be when you have family, friends, and pets all together in some celebration. Or, it may be when you are in a renovation and you step back in appreciation. Or, you may have a sighting of Nature in which everything comes together in awe of some inner harmony, in which you are part of a larger whole.

You often see fulfillment in the play of children (or your own play). When you see them play, they are in a test of their abilities, concentration and focus, enjoying others, and have a total involvement in something they <u>love</u> to do. No matter what the level of their skill, a child must pursue play, something they can't do without.

At work, there may have been a most enjoyable challenge, and you pursued it for its own sake. Just being in the path of discovery and involvement was satisfying. You didn't have to "arrive" to feel fulfillment. You went from uncertainty to mastery.

In all fulfillments, we experience an ease and acceptance, even in difficulty, in which all we do comes together. Our needs, our goal, our involvement, our skills, the benefit to ourselves, the cheer of others, and more. We feel more together, more real.

Can we agree that fulfillment is not the symbols of happiness we are sold? Wealth, status, power, fame, consumerism, or the next big thing, all are about how others feel about us, not actually how we feel about ourselves or how we experience life.

Have you met others who are on the Fulfilling path? They are not splashy. They seem to have loving-kindness for the whole world and go from one absorbing activity to another with ease and little fanfare. They always seem to be into something that has much meaning for them. You relax with them and feel you can be yourself. They are often unheralded and unsung.

Gardening is a fulfillment for so many, and is actually our most widely shared hobby. While the goal may be healthy food or ornament, all the steps of preparing, planting, cultivating, nurturing, and harvesting are satisfying in themselves. Each involves a challenge, skills, and absorbing attention. This humble pursuit can be fulfilling, from beginning to end.

The climber of sheer rock faces is totally absorbed in each toehold and grip along the way. The world falls away. The climber brings all his/her skills and knowledge to each step. Each moment is timeless. At the end of the climb, the exhilaration is real. The climber has gone through fear and arrives at courage.

The mystic, or "near-death," experience has been shown to visit over 30% of adults (Pew Research, 2003). In this, you experience being drawn to and being part of a Universal Love, a life-altering experience that leads many to leave their everyday ambitions and adopt a life of compassion (Ring, 2008).

Each of these experiences of fulfillment seems to originate in love, our complete involvement in something we truly care about. Compassion itself embodies a uniquely human purpose that can make us care about all living creatures and even feel a stewardship for the earth itself. This has not been given to other living beings.

As you can see, there is no one way. These examples only hint at the breadth of fulfilling experiences. Almost any arena of life can be fulfilling.

Research Views on Happiness

What did the writers of the Constitution mean by the pursuit of happiness? In our time, it has come to refer to all kinds of impulses, appetites, attractions, beliefs, cults, fads, consumer goods, disciplines – you name it – all promising happiness with a big, toothy smile. These do not last, have little lasting meaning and can be traps in themselves. It would take a thick catalogue to list all of these wonders. Here instead, I will summarize the views of scientists who have researched happiness.

Siegal (2010) feels that "mindset" underlies happy people. This means that all "domains" of thought tend toward a coherent sense of Self. Movements away from integration lead to less emotional well-being.

When your sense of Self expands, you may have a life of meaning and purpose. This highly intellectual approach to happiness does not describe concretely how to do this.

Lipton (2005), a biologist, feels that the choice we have of either instinctive action or reflective action is the foundation of free will: "the conscious mind's capacity to override the subconscious mind's preprogrammed behaviors." To "thrive," we need more than the protection afforded by instincts. We also need growth, e.g. to "actively seek joyful, loving, fulfilling lives that stimulate growth." Growth provides energy; protection uses energy.

Csikszentmihalyi (1990) finds happiness lies in "flow," an experience of investing energy in consciously chosen challenges and goals, so that we both enjoy and grow with them. For this, we don't set goals at the start, but by pursuing each challenge for its own sake we find a "meaningful pattern." In time, our consciousness focuses our attention and builds a hierarchy of our goals. "Flow" brings joy by concentrating on clear goals, with immediate feedback, deep involvement, skill, and sheer amount of time. We acquire a new, expanded sense of our Self.

Haidt (2006) concludes happiness is getting a balance, or coherence, between these three areas of life: work, love, and "something larger." In work, we have a basic need for competence and mastery in some field. We also have a need for an attachment or bond with a lifelong partner. In feeling part of something greater than ourselves, we transcend ordinary concerns and grow larger ourselves. These basic needs loosely correspond to the hierarchy of needs in Maslow's model for personal growth.

Seligman (2002) concludes that "Happiness comes in many routes. Looked at this way, it becomes our life task to display our signature strengths and virtues in the major realms of living: work, love, parenting and finding purpose. The full life consists of experiencing positive emotions about the past and future...and using these strengths in the service of something larger to obtain meaning."

The Growth of Self from Emotional Fulfillment

You probably have noticed that these reviewers have connected the growth and expansion of the Self with happiness. Indeed, only human beings, among all the animals, have the capacity to reflect consciously and make decisions that do not follow instincts. We call this wondrous capacity the Self. As we develop, this sense of the Self takes on a reality of its own and makes its own claims. And, as Maslow (1962) asserts, after we have met our basic needs for safety, belonging and affection, the Self has a need to grow to its full potential, or "self-actualization." Most everyone tries to get beyond purely basic needs to the larger ones: the well-being of the family, of the community, of humanity, or even the whole of life.

The unique purpose of emotions for humans, contrary to the instincts of animals, is to fulfill our sense of Self. This is not "selfish" in the sense of narrow survival needs, but the sense of a vibrant, purposeful Self. This sense of Self is with you wherever you go and is even dearer to you than your emotions. Your sense of Self tells you who you are. And what you do with your emotions goes to the heart of who you are. In other words, for humans, emotions serve your sense of Self and what makes you happy.

Happiness from Emotional Fulfillment

So how does the choice of how we fulfill our emotions lead to happiness and a sure sense of one's Self?

Recall that each emotion originates in a relation we have to something or someone we care about or love. The more we care, the more intense the emotion. Each emotion reveals our relation to a barrier or threat to our love object, or the relation we have when in contact with our love object. Both the "negative" and the positive emotions can bring us closer to our loves. The diagram below will make this clear:

(-) Emotion	Barrier to Love-object	(+) Emotion	Contact with Love-object
Fear	Threat	Curiosity	Understanding
Anger	Frustration	Awe	Inspiration
Hurt	Harm	Love	Identify with
Envy	Left out	Humor	Acceptance
Sadness	Missing	Empathy	Feeling for
Loneliness	Unlovable		
Shynessl	Separation		
Insecurity	Helpless		
Disgust	Tainted		

Even while there are more basic emotions on the "barrier" side, all can lead to contact, or fulfillment, depending on how you act on them. These "negative" emotions alert you clearly that you need to overcome the obstacle or threat to what you care about. When fulfilled, each emotion brings you closer to a vibrant, integrated sense of yourself and happiness.

Love, the Goal of all Emotions

It may be easy to accept, in an intuitive sense, that all emotions reveal your relation to something or someone you care about, the strongest feelings being for what you truly love most. But the search and discovery of what you love most can be a long and winding road.

To begin with, you have many counterfeits of love that distract you from your true loves. Your appetites, urges, fads, cults, consumerism, addictions, boredom, and a thousand other cultural seductions push and pull you around. You may have earnestly followed the lead of others to what will bring happiness. You may have even read the self-help literature or attended the seminars on happiness. Even then, the emotion of your vital love is elusive, as it is more like a gentle tide that pulls you softly rather than like the bite and force of the other emotions.

In addition, surprisingly, love can flow towards anything: a lifelong interest, a true friend, a skill, all forms of life, and even the whole of life itself. You have only your own experiences and the feelings that go with them to confirm your love. No one can tell you what or who you love or ought to love. Love comes from your very own nature – your temperament, interests, abilities, skills, experience – your nature selects it from everything else. When you find your love, you are accepting and humble before it.

There is no one way to discover your loves. And many discover them only by their mid-30's, according to one study, after you have experienced a lot of life. But several types of experiences have been found to be most helpful in realizing what you care about most (Sher, 2003). These are also drawn from the clinical literature and my own experience with my clients.

> Peak experiences of satisfaction, when everything seemed to come together
> The childhood play that you were most consistently attracted to.
> In viewing a movie, seeing a satisfying role to play in life
> A promise to yourself that someday you would try out something
> An ideal work or play or person that appears in your daydreaming
> Some activity you return to over and gain for its appeal to you
> Someone you can't get out of your mind
> A lifelong interest you return to whenever you get the chance

When you find your loves and bring them into your life every day, you find where you belong in life and what gives most meaning. You take satisfaction every step of your path and don't require medals or applause to confirm your importance. You are less vulnerable to the setbacks and pain of everyday existence. You delight in bringing all of your interests, understanding, skill and experience in your act of love. You don't need a final finish, because the subject of your love is ever growing and expansive, and you expand along with it. Your love is all encompassing and much bigger than you. You are humble and happy to follow your love wherever it leads, knowing you are a vital part of something larger. If you are fortunate in your life circumstances, your loves may be a balance of your work, your life partner, and your larger cause.

This happy state has been named in many ways, reflecting the vastness of the whole subject of love.
Flow, following your bliss, being centered, the path of wisdom, self-actualization, joy, compassion, transformation of self, balance, nirvana, spirituality and even the mystic experience – all capture some aspect of your immersion into the whole of your love.

Virtue from Emotional Fulfillment

Have you noticed that the outcome for handling each emotion in an integrative way, leading to fulfillment, sounds a lot like a virtue? Virtues are defined as traits of a good character: moral strength, honor, or goodness. Seligman (2002) noticed that character and morality have been slighted by science, and formed a group study of over 200 religious and philosophic traditions. He found 6 basic virtues and 24 personal "strengths" in this vast literature. The 6 virtues he found are: wisdom, justice, temperance, humanity, courage and transcendence. Notice how in the following table the fulfillment of each emotion describes some aspect of each of the 6 virtues:

Emotion	Action needed	Entrapment	Fulfillment	6 related virtues
Fear	Face up	Oppression	Courage	Courage
Anger	Assert needs	Bitterness	Satisfaction	Temperance
Sadness	Reflect goals	Despair	Hopefulness	Transcendence
Shyness	Play a part	Alienation	Belonging	Justice

Hurt	Healing	Withdrawal	Forgiveness	Humanity
Envy	Value	Greed	Gratitude	Wisdom
Disgust	Evaluate	Shame	Fairness	Justice
Awe	Embrace whole	Narrowness	Largeness	Transcendence
Insecure	Care for self	Dependence	Self reliance	Temperance
Jealousy	Release other	Uncertainty	Affirmation	Humanity
Love	Engagement	Coldness	Compassion	Humanity
Humor	See incongruity	Pessimism	Acceptance	Temperance
Curiosity	Explore	Close-minded	Open-minded	Wisdom
Empathy	Feel for	Distance	Closeness	Humanity

Happiness as an Emotion

If the purpose of emotional fulfillment is to complete the emotions and be free of them, what is left?
Is happiness an emotion? Even with love as fulfillment and purpose of all the other emotions, what is that state of body, feelings, appraisal, neurology, urge to act, belief and health that defines a basic emotion? What do you feel when all your emotional needs are met, even love?

"Contentment" doesn't have much curb appeal; it sounds even a bit stale. "Peaceful" doesn't sound sexy, either. How about the feeling of beauty, goodness, gratitude, charity for all and universal love? They can sound both naïve and difficult, at the same time. Do we have the language to describe the contentment that comes from emotional fulfillment?

The "happiness" I refer to is a transformative, dynamic and life-changing feeling. It means you see that world as good in spite of your hardships; you see beauty in everything and are astonished; you see how much to be grateful for despite your deprivations. You accept all the emotion in the tears that come to your eyes at a good deed or a happy ending. Your whole body, not just a part, becomes transformed into something lighter, freer, and unrestrained. An inexpressible lightness of being. Your health becomes optimal in all its measures: appetite, heart, immunity, vital energy, balance, longevity. You appraise the past, present and future with optimism and see the good in everyone. Your beliefs are not naïve, but hard-won and the truth as you know it. You have seen the truth through glasses neither dark nor rose-tinted. You see peace as a dynamic process of meeting your needs and emotions and those of others, and keep that vital balance everyday in your engagement with your loves.

Chapter 8: Emotions in Family, Community and Nation

Emotions not only energize and motivate your individual life, but also group life. Advertising and the media consciously push their audiences. The appeals of a leader or charismatic speaker are often to your emotions. Crowds themselves can immerse you in a swell of shared emotion, whether through music, games, parades, protest, and more. Our representatives in government are themselves motivated by emotions, and may follow instinctive paths even as they bear great responsibility. Whole communities and even nations can be said to have a common mood that flows from its history, customs and common concerns.

This overview must be brief and selective. When you stir in 14 basic emotions into the complex stew of social life, you find the vast literature of human history. At the same time, it is broadly helpful to recognize how emotions drive our family, community and social life. The dominant and recruited emotions help you see where the events, drama and players are coming from, especially the key players who make the decisions that put the action into play.

So rather than anything like a comprehensive review of the emotions in social life, I offer samples from varied sources: from clinical literature, current events, history and many other accounts.

Emotions in family life

Families are probably more unlike each other than races, languages, tribes or nations. The reality TV series "Wife Swap" shows vividly how the emotional life of one family can dominate their activities and beliefs, and be so opposite and unlike that of another. In each episode, wives "swapped" families, agreeing to follow explicit family rules for two weeks, before attempting to change them. One family had irresistible fears about dirt, contamination and strangers and severely limited their social life and the play of their children. The other family had an especially strong need to belong and participate, and were involved in a continual parade of festivities, performances, and rallies, with a riot of costumes. The charm of this series was that whole families would borrow and adapt some practices of the "opposite" family that were missing in their own. In the end, both families expressed gratitude for the other in bringing more balance into their family lives.

The dominant emotions in American family life are amazingly varied. In some rural areas the anger of broken dreams and disillusionment is seen in a hard-bitten way of life and resistance to outsiders (Bageant, 2007). In some mountain areas, there is instant kindness and concern in some families that allows for tolerance and openness to strangers. Some families have a strong need to belong, and form a loyal, bonded extended family that may live only a few miles away at most. Other families share a sense of insecurity and members need to prove themselves, to the extent that members are overreaching and ambitious. In every family the predominant emotions are reinforced and validated by its members and hardened into shared attitudes and beliefs.

Emotions in Community Life

The yet-unnamed emotion in the "need to belong" drives the sentiments of loyalty to one's school, neighborhood and community. The bonds of loyalty and empathy demand allegiance and conformity to festivities, observances, and social events. This powerful emotion can recruit the emotion of disgust and even anger at a practice or way of life that is much unlike that of one's own community. Questioning the loyalty to foods, clothing, recreation, housing and so on can lead to hostility. There may be little empathy for other practices, which can seem shallow, even contemptible. "They're different" can conceal a tangle of strong emotions.

In cities, neighborhoods can exist side-by-side which have great differences in status, access and values. In poor sections where you struggle day by day for necessities, the emotions of insecurity, fear and anger can team up in the form of defiance and protest. In the hoods, street gangs may seem like the best way to get protection, some security and a sense of belonging all at once. On the other hand, in the same cities, neighborhoods may mingle easily in public games, large parks and public events, or at beaches and recreational facilities. Breaking the ice and getting acquainted is comfortable then, and allows a person's natural curiosity and warmth to come into play.

Putnam (2000) has documented how membership in every group, from Rotary to bowling leagues, has dropped by around 50% in the last 35 years. The two major reasons for this are, in his analysis, TV and the media and the crushing pressure of two-worker families. This also makes for "latch key" children who can develop loneliness and diffuse anger. Parents are known to overindulge their children out of the guilt about their absence. On the other hand, parents also choose neighborhoods where schools, activities and other parents can provide the "village" children need. In doing this parents and children both can find the role they want in this community for their vital interests and emotional needs.

In our schools, students complain of boredom, frustration and of seeing nothing of themselves in what they are taught. Yet even in the most disadvantaged of schools, the building of a community of parents, teachers and mentors all acting together, as well as the building of character, have been key to remarkable turnarounds (Leppzer,2010).

Even those who are most alienated from the larger community form "outsider" groups, such as cults, bicycle gangs, special interest groups.

Even cults and terrorist groups can offer a great sense of importance to a "spoiled life" according to Hoffer (1951). In schools, students are adept at forming outsider groups that satisfy both the need to belong and be special, like Goths, freaks, Rebels, Nerds and more. "Attitude" may reflect persistent, hardened moods that are born of anger and frustration.

Then again, a wealth of opportunity exists in your community for immersing you in your vital interests and loves. In online sources of meet-ups, you find hundreds of groups active with similar interests, from crafts and sports to readings and discussion. Community colleges and some universities have courses with wide appeal and usefulness, sometimes for credit. The internet itself can open doors and make contact for meeting emotional needs, especially the emotions of curiosity, belonging, and insecurity. Volunteer groups help satisfy feelings of compassion and empathy for sick or needy persons.

Emotions in the Life of the Nation

The well-being, happiness, or mood of the nation has become the center of recent attention. Recognizing that Gross National Product is not a reliable measure, many kinds of surveys in government and out have begun to measure national well-being. They measure everything from daily mood ratings to hand-held rating devices. Some even analyze song lyrics, blogs and State of the Union speeches. One author (Woods, 2009) who looked at many aspects of pop culture has documented the growth of anger in our national life.

The mood of a whole nation is not set so much by one event or set of events as much as by how others respond. The TV and news media are in a key place to form attitudes and feelings towards events, whether by the opinions of "talking heads" or the selective reporting of events. If the attitude shown is cynicism, then anger and disgust are activated. Shock and alarm at events evoke fear. Many emotions can be aroused and sustained, and after time, develop into a more hardened mood shared by our national life.

The leaders in a nation, either in representative office or in public opinion, are especially powerful in shaping our emotional stance towards our problems. They may blame and accuse (anger, disgust), sound dire warnings (fear) appeal to accountability (insecurity, empathy) or to patriotism and shared values (need to belong). Your heightened emotions help you remember these appeals and support the related attitudes and need for action. The leaders themselves may be driven more by instinctual needs than reflection.

The relations between nations is fraught with strong emotions, partly because of our own vital concerns and partly because we don't have the check of direct experience of another nation. Following Maslow (1997), at the start we may be more concerned with safety, trust, and common interests, than with developing mutual bonds and appreciation. The feelings related to war, transgressions, or betrayal can last for generations as they are preserved in the collective memory and narrative. The resolution by means of forgiveness, reconciliation, negotiation, gratitude and shared interests are fulfilling paths that take determined effort in the face of the enduring feelings or moods of a nation. There is emerging hope that global empathy will be energized by a highly interconnected world through the internet and other agencies (Rifkin, 2009). "From belongings to belonging."

Epilogue – The Next Step

This book may have seemed conceptually broad and ambitious in attempting to survey the vast landscape of emotional life. There has been an abundance of concepts and new terms that may make you feel that the meaning has escaped you. Then again, it may also seem intuitively right to others who may feel, "I already knew this somehow." Still others may wonder how to put such a thorough-going integration of emotions into action. You may think, "Sounds great, but how do you bring it off?"

In answer, my fondest wish is that the model for emotional fulfillment has been acceptable, understandable, and embraceable, especially for its hopefulness and direction. This short reading has been an attempt to describe a far-reaching model of emotional development and purpose. However, it does not directly demonstrate its usefulness to your life, as it alludes only in general terms to the concrete action steps that are needed to integrate emotions

To meet these needs, I have authored a series of short, readable self-help books. Each describes the action needed to integrate a single emotion in gradual, clear steps, using self-tests, check-lists, examples, and related readings. The Emotional Fulfillment Series embraces the 14 basic emotions. Each self-help book embodies both my professional experience with the lives of my clients, as well as the best literature, not only in psychological research, but also in related disciplines. To date, the Ebooks covering **Anger, Loneliness**, and **Shyness** have been published.

In these Ebooks, those who feel troubled by loneliness, anger, anxiety, depression, insecurity, shyness, sadness, and more, will get a call to immediate action. As you acquire new experience in trying out new attitudes and action, your very experience will persuade you to incorporate these changes into your life. The series of gradually, doable steps will help you adopt them as your own. You will see that they work for you. They become your new habits.

Therapists of every orientation will also see the applicability of the model to his/her professional work. Emotions have been woven in and out of most formal schools of psychotherapy without ever having much standing or purpose of their own. Most counselors will integrate emotional needs into their practice with ease and understanding through the Emotional Fulfillment Series, which offer both brief testing and graduated homework. The Model is not meant to be a new school of psychotherapy but a means of bringing the clarity and power of emotions to fruition in every school. A facilitator, not a new order.

For more serious readers, the much larger book, **Emotional Fulfillment**, expands the model and has a chapter for each of the 14 basic emotions. Over 400 citations are grounded in the best research and clinical literature. Additional chapters on education, morality and therapy demonstrate applications of the model.

How the Emotional Fulfillment Series came to be.

What is the Emotional Fulfillment Series of Ebooks ?

These Ebooks are clear, well-founded guides to handling all of your 14 basic emotions in a way that fulfills them and completes them, rather than handling them in a self-defeating, destructive way that perpetuates them. The book you are holding describes the Model for how emotional fulfillment works.

In the Series you will find your emotions are your faithful friends, always looking out for your well-being, and not necessarily something to trip you up and cause trouble. Emotions express your essential needs, and when you fulfill them, you find the possibility of love in your life, and the return of peace. As your relation to each emotion grows in each Ebook, you will trust yourself with more and more compassion, and wish the same for everyone. In each Ebook you learn to transform the upset and hardship of each emotion into fulfillment. You acquire not only a sense of mastery and a positive view of yourself, but also a kind of spiritual energy.

The origination of the Series

The beginning of the Ebooks was simply a shoebox, a stack of 5x8 cards, each one describing how a counselor helps a client change. In this way I was trying to break away from abstract schools of psychotherapy taught in graduate school. I soon saw that, no matter what technique I used, the client's motivation was always essential – and the emotional push behind it.

Then, in 1977, I was moved by a seminar given by Dr. Hans Seyle (1956) whose model for the body's reaction to the stress of disease, the Shock – Defense – Exhaustion stages, seemed a vital model for the development of emotions over time. At the same time, a passage from

Krishnamurti's Commentaries (1952) sketched out the development of anger as Anger – Resentment – Bitterness. Together, these had an immediate, moving impact on me.

In August, 1978, I wrote down what would become a life plan, entitled "Ideas about becoming expert in emotions." It listed all the disciplines I would need to study, collaborations I needed with staff and graduate students, needed research, and even publishing a basic book on each emotion. The latter, much later, would become the Series of Ebooks. The life plan would also lead to a well-researched and clinically sound book on the purpose of emotions.

The development of the Series

Soon, I began writing my reflections on my therapy clients' lifelong history of dealing with the basic emotions. This binder, called "Reflections" grew into several binders. This charting of the progress of emotions was not only stimulating, but also useful to my clinical work. I formed a community counseling center that was both service and research oriented, with deep community roots.

In the early 80's, partly through the emergence of health psychology through Pelletier (1988) and others, I realized that I had focused mostly on the negative side of emotions, the pathology. I found a positive model in an area I was starting to specialize in – anxiety and phobias. In the cognitive-behavioral model of treating panic, you gradually faced up to your fears using calming methods, and found freedom from panic rather than its opposite, oppression by panic. I began developing models for how each of the primary emotions could lead to a either a positive outcome, or a negative outcome.

The maturation of the Series

The next several years were a time of much study of a wide range of literature, from philosophy and cultural history, to basic science and clinical research. Seminars, conferences, graduate students, and my own research provided a tighter focus on emotions. The writings by Lazarus, Izard, Young and Ekman (year?) were especially relevant. By 2000, I had formulated the model fairly completely: the three stages of emotional development, one in the instinctive path, the other in the fulfilling path. I was continually surprised that these two paths led to very opposite end-states and had such basic implications, not only for psychotherapy, but also for education and morality. By 2004, it seemed clear that each emotion had a uniquely human purpose and meaning that was a transformation of the emotion itself.

In 2006, a serious illness, since cured, compelled me to look at what I loved and mattered most to me, and I immediately determined to finish my life work of over 30 years. While the scope of the model and the larger book has expanded greatly, it has been a most satisfying companion for all it has demanded of me. In turn, the writings and publications of many authors, clinicians and researchers have become as friends who have offered the very best of themselves and their work to me. Even then, without my clients who have poured out their lives to me, there would have been no inspiration. For all I have a world of gratitude.

Citations

Alim, T. et al. Trauma, resilience and recovery in a high-risk African-American population. American J. Psychiatry, 2008. 1566-1575.

Bageant, J. Deer Hunting with Jesus. Crown Publishing, 2007.

Beck, A. et al. Cognitive theories of Depression. Guilford, 1974.

Berlyne, D. Conflict, Arousal and Curiosity. McGraw-Hill, 1960

Bonanno, G. & Keltner, D. Facial expressions of emotion. Journal of Abnormal Psychology, 1997. 126-137. Bonanno, G. Resilience to Loss and Chronic Grief. J. of Personality and Social Psychology, 2002.1150-64.

Bonanno, G. Loss, trauma and human resilience. American Psychologist, 2004. 20-28.

Bonnano, G. The Other Side of Sadness. Basic Books, 2009.

Bonanno, G. & Field, N. Examining the delayed grief hypothesis across five years of bereavement. American Behavioral Scientist, 2001. 778-806.

Brown,D. Human uhiversals. Temple U., 1991.

Christ, G. Healing Children's Grief. Oxford U., 2000.

Clore et al. Effective causes and consequences of social information processing. In Wyn, R. & Snull. (Eds.) Handbook of social cognition. Erebaum, 1994.

Csikszentmihalyi, M. Flow: the Psychology of Optimal Experience. Harper Collins, 1990.

D'amazio, A. Looking for Spinoza. Harcourt Books, 2003.

D'amazio, A. Descartes Error. G.P.Putnam, 1994.

Davis, L. Empathy. Brown and Benchmark, 1994.

Decety, J. & Ickes, W. The Social Neuroscience of Empathy. MIT, 2009.

Ekman, P. Expression and the nature of emotion. In, Scherer, K. & Ekman, P. (Eds.) Approaches to emotion. Erebaum, 1984.

Ekman, P. The Nature of Emotion. Oxford U. Press, 1994.

Forgas, J. Mood and judgment: the affect infusion model. Psychological Bulletin, 1993. 39-66.

Forgas, J. & Bower, G. Mood Effects on Person, Perception and Judgment. J. Personality and Social Psychology, 1987. 53-60.

Freud, S. Civilization and its Discontents. ....1930.

Frija, N., The Emotions, Cambridge U., 1986.

Frija, N. & Mesquita, B. in Emotions and beliefs. Cambridge U. Press, 2000.

Frija, N., Manstead, A., & Bem, S. (eds.) Emotions and Beliefs. Cambridge U. Press, 2000.

Haidt, J. The Happiness Hypothesis. Basic Books, 2006.

Heidegger, M. Being and Time. SUNY, 2010.

Hoermann et al 2005

Isen, A. Positive affect, cognitive processes and social behavior. In Berkowitz, L. (Ed.) Advances in experimental social psychology. Academic Press, 1987.

Hoffer, E. The True Believer. Harper & Row, 1951.

Izard, C. Human Emotions. Plenum Press, 1986.

Izard, C. Basic emotions, relations among emotions, and emotion-cognition relations. Psychological Review, 1992. 561-5.

James, W. The varieties of Religious Experience. Longmans, Green & Co., 1902

Kaga, Reziak & Suidian, 1988

Keltman, S. & Bonanno, G. A study of Laughter and Dissociation. J. of Personality and Social Psychology, 1997. 687-702.

Konston, D. Pity transformed. Duckworth, 2001.

Krishnamurti, J. Commentaries on living. Quest Books, 1952.

Kubla-Ross, S. On Death and Dying, Routledge, 1973

Kupfer, D. et al. A research agenda for DSMV. American Psychiatric Publications, 2002.

Lazarus, R. Emotion and Adaptation. Oxford U. Press, 1991.

Lazarus, R. Stress and emotion.. Springer, 1999.

Levenson, R. Autonomic specificity and emotion. In Davidson, et al (Eds.) Handbook of affective science. Oxford U., 2003.

Leppzer, R. Beating the Odds (DVD). Turning Tide Productions, 2010.

Levethal, H. & Patrick-Miller L. Emotions and illness: the mind is in the body. In Lerves, M. & Haviland, J. (eds.) Handbook of emotions. Guilford Press, 1993.

Lipton, B. The Biology of Belief. Mountain of Love, 2005.

Maslow, A, Toward a psychology of being. VanNostrand, 1962.

Maslow, A. Motivation and Personality. Pearson, 1997.

McDougall, W. Outline of Psychology. Scribner, 1923.

Meichenbaum, D. Treating adults with PTSD. Institute Press, 1994.

Nickerson, R. et al, In Decety,J. & Ickes, W. (Eds.) The social science of empathy. MIT, 2009.

Oatle, K. & Johnson-Laird, P. Towards a cognitive theory of emotions. Cognition and emotions, 1987. 29-50.

Oatley, K. Emotions, a Brief History. Blackwell, 2004.

Oatly, K. Keltner, D. & Jenkins, J. Understanding emotions. Blackwell, 2006.

Panksepp, J. Affective Neuroscience: the Foundations of Human and Animal Emotions. Oxford U, 1998.

Psychology, 1984. 53-60.

Pelletier, K. Holistic Medicine, Delta, 1988

Petrie, Booth & Pennebaker. J. Personality and Social Psychology, 1998. 1264-1272.

Pew Research, 2003

Plutchik, R. Emotions in the Practice of Psychotherapy APA, 2008.

Putnam, R. Bowling Alone. Touchstone, 2000.

Rifkin, J. The Empathic Civilization. Penguin group, 2009.

Ring, K. Mindset. iUniverse, 2008.

Roseman,L. Cognitive determinants of emotion: a structural theory. In Shaver, P. (Ed.) Review of Personality and Social Psychology, Vol. 5. Sage, 1984.

Seligman, M. Authentic Happiness. Free Press, 2002.

Seyle, H. The Stress of Life. McGraw-Hill, 1956.

Shaver, P. Wu, S. & Schwartz, J. Cross-cultural similarities and differences in emotion and its regulation. In Clark, S. (ED.) Review of Personality and Social Psychology, Emotion. Sage, 1992. 175-212.

Sher, B. WIshcraft. Ballantine Books, 2003.

Siegel, D. Mindset. Bantam,, 2010.

Sorabji, R. Emotion and peace of mind. Oxford U Press, 2000.

Storbeck & Clore. With sadness comes accuracy. Psychological Science, 2005. 785-791.

Stroebe, M. & Shut, H. The Dual Process of Coping with Bereavement. Death Studies, 1999. 197-224.

Tesser et al. In Krienick, J. & Petty, R. (Eds.) Attitude strength: antecedents and consequences. Erebaum, 1995.

Thompson, A. & Meyer, S. In Gross, J. (Ed.) Handbook of emotional regulation. Gilford, 2007.

Tomkins, S. Affect, imagery, Consciousness. Springer, 1962.

Torgensen, S. Epidemeology. In Oldham J. et al (Eds.) The American Psychiatric Publishing Textbook of personality disorders. American Psychiatric Publications, 2005.

Watson, D. & Clark, L. Emotions, Moods and Temperaments. In Ekman, P & Davison, J. (Eds.) The Nature of Emotion. Oxford U., 1994.

Woods, P. A Bee in the Mouth. Encounter Books, 2006.

Young, J. & Klosko, J. Reinventing Your Life. Plume, 1994.

Young, J.Klosko, J. & Weishaar, M. Schema therapy. Guilford Press,, 2003.

Zautra, A. Emotions, Stress, and Health. Oxford U., 2003.